How To Write
A BOOK THIS WEEKEND,
Even If You Flunked
English Like I Did

Vic Johnson

Laurenzana Press

Published by:

Laurenzana Press
PO Box 1220
Melrose, FL 32666 USA

www.LaurenzanaPress.com

****

ISBN-13: 978-1-937918-73-6

FREE Report

405 Ideas for Powerful Titles.
Download from TitleIdeas.com

CONTENTS

Introduction

You *can* **write a book this weekend**. How can I be so certain? Because the book you're reading now was written in a weekend. And the techniques I used to do it are easily duplicatable by anyone who follows these simple instructions.

For 30 years or more I wanted to write a book, and I think many others – *USA Today* says as many as 82% – also share that dream. But every time I'd think about writing a book I'd conjure an image of Ernest Hemingway pounding away on his Corona 3 typewriter in the wee hours of the morning, accompanied by his ever-present half-empty bottle of scotch. So that was always a block to me, because I never could see myself doing that.

Fortunately I came up with an alternative, which is what I'm going to share with you here.

Why I'm Qualified to Write This Book

The biggest reason is because I've actually done what I'm teaching here. I've done it successfully and I've done it more than once. At the risk of sounding immodest, my success would say I'm an 'expert' in how to do it.

If it helps you in any way to believe that you can do what I've done, let me also point out that I flunked English in college. Many of my sentences end in prepositions, which I guess is a no-no. I'm prone to use a lot of slang and put commas in the wrong places – if I use them at all. But I try to communicate as if I'm physically speaking to my reader. And since I'm a true Southern boy, my grammar is decidedly at odds with educators and those who think language is more about style than substance.

I didn't arrive at this point without my share of obstacles and heartbreaks. Seventeen years ago I wasn't getting ready to write a book in a weekend. I was packing up my belongings after a judge evicted us from our home and gave us just 48 hours to find another place to live, even though we had nowhere to go and no money.

A year later our last automobile was repossessed, and I had made a whopping $14,027 for the year, which placed our family of five below the federal poverty level. (I've since earned more money than that in a month from my books, which has never been more than a part-time effort.)

Altogether I've authored eight books (I use the term 'authored' instead of 'written,' because none of them were written in the traditional sense that one associates with book writers, like my earlier example of Hemingway). One of my books has sold more than 75,000 copies, and has been translated into Japanese, Czech, Slovak and Farsi. One has been the number one book on goal-setting at Amazon, and still comes up number one and number two when people search that term at Amazon.

I've had several books that reached the coveted top 100 overall at Amazon. And at times I've out-ranked such well-known celebrities as Colin Powell, Warren Buffett, Mark Cuban, Tim Ferris and many others.

At this writing I'm a top 100 business author, and a top 100 author in advice and how-to at Amazon, and have been for quite some time. I've done it all without writing in the traditional way that most people think authors write.

And *you* can too!

Will This Technique Work With Any Kind of Topic?

It probably will, but it might need some modifications to use it for writing in the fiction niches. (I'm not a fiction writer, so I don't know everything involved with producing those kinds of works.)

But I can say with absolute certainty that it will work with any kind of non-fiction book, though I don't believe you could complete large works like a biography of Churchill in a weekend or even several weekends.

Non-fiction books tend to deliver information rather than entertainment, though it can certainly help to deliver the information in an entertaining fashion.

How-to information books are primarily what I focus on. While the average novel might be somewhere in the range of 80,000 to 100,000 words or more, my publishing company has produced more than 50 how-to books in the 12,000 to 20,000 word range. So I'm really a big believer in how-to books and delivering information.

Now there are some definite advantages to how-to books. First, you don't have to have or research any specific knowledge to write a how-to book. It's as simple as finding one or more experts in that field and interviewing them.

A friend of mine, Mike Litman, did just that and created a bestselling book called <u>Conversations With Millionaires</u>. Mike was broke at the time he did the interviews with people like Wally Amos, founder of Famous Amos Cookies; Jim McCann, founder of 1-800 Flowers; Mark Victor Hansen, co-creator of the *Chicken Soup* book series, and many others. He turned the transcripts of those interviews into a book, and that was the beginning of a seven-figure business for him.

You could also take a reporter's approach to writing how-to books. Reporters aren't normally experts in the fields they're writing on, but they gather and organize the information and knowledge, and present it in a way that enables the reader to understand that information.

(By the way, it's not a wise idea to present yourself as an

expert if you're not. If you're not wealthy, don't write how to become wealthy books pretending you know the secrets. But it's okay to report how others became wealthy.)

The classic book, <u>Think and Grow Rich</u> by Napoleon Hill, was written in 1937. The basis of that book is interviews Napoleon Hill did with 500 of America's wealthiest people at the time. When he started he was just a poor reporter – that was his training and his background. But he was able to get the interviews with these people, and out of that came several of his big works, the biggest by far being <u>Think and Grow Rich</u>. So it's not necessary that you be an expert in your area of interest.

How-to readers are looking for specific information in a reasonably easy to read format. Your work doesn't need to be the next Pulitzer Prize winner; however, you do want to present it with fairly good grammar and English (that's what good editors are for). It's not critical that it be the compelling type of literature people are going to talk about at the country club or beauty salon.

Since readers are looking more for information than entertainment, it's okay – and even preferred – to deliver the information in the most concise and direct manner. That's why you can turn out one with as few as 12,000 words, and I've even seen some good ones in the 7,500 word range. People often ask me the question, "Vic, how long should it be?" And I answer, "It should be just long enough to deliver all the information."

Bear in mind that if you've got a very short book it had

better contain some really good content. I've paid as much as $97 for a book that only had 16 pages, but they were 16 very *powerful* pages containing incredible information and a lot of takeaways. I also paid a couple of bucks for books that had 200 and 300 pages, but I couldn't find one thing I could say added value to my life.

You're not selling potatoes or corn or something like that by the pound, and you're not selling your book by the number of words. But it will help the reader's perception to know your work has enough substance that they're going to be getting their money's worth.

Many information books contain just 12,000 to 20,000 words, and deliver the content people are looking for. If they walk away feeling they received a significant amount of added value to their life, then you've succeeded and you're going to have a popular book.

Most how-to books have a long shelf life (I talk elsewhere about evergreen books, and how-to books definitely fit that description). Me personally? I'm all about doing the work once and earn money from it over a long period of time, and how-to books help me accomplish that.

Why a Weekend Works Well to Write a Book

First of all, it's easier to focus on a weekend and you can work uninterrupted. Once you're in the zone you don't have to stop. If you're working during the week you may only have an hour or so available. But a weekend gives you a much longer time to get into the "flow" or in the "zone," and you can be very productive.

You know the feeling I'm talking about: When your production is at an incredibly high level, and things appear to be coming out of you with little or no effort, is the 'zone' you want to achieve when you're writing your book. And I find it's easier to do that on a weekend.

A weekend has its own natural deadline. In most parts of the world a weekend ends on Sunday night, so you'll know when it's over. You'll know what you're working against. It's like having a timeclock in a sporting match, and all weekend you're constantly working against that time. And you can do so in a manner that's not tense or nerve-wracking; but it does keep you motivated and driven.

Find a quiet place where the chance for interruption is minimal as you really want to be able to focus only on your book, and you don't want to have any other distractions.

You want to **get physically comfortable**. I like to sit in my easy chair rather than at my desk. When I sit at my desk I feel like I'm more task-oriented, so that's where I sit when I need to get specific tasks done. When I'm sitting in my easy chair and I've got some music on, then I'm a lot more creative than I would be in my office.

Which leads me to my next point: **Put music on in the background** that will help you create, like some good jazz or classical music. I created a channel at Pandora that plays what I call "spa music," which I let run constantly in the background. It seems to help my creativity, and I know it does with other people as well. Now I love hard rock – especially classic hard rock. But not when I'm creating, as it's harder to get into that same creative mode, at least for me.

Turn the phones off! You can check your voicemail for emergencies when you take a break. But try not to get involved in a conversation until you're done for the weekend since you're trying to avoid any type of distraction.

Don't turn the 'spigot' off until you absolutely have to! When things start flowing, don't stop. When you're in the flow, you need to stay in the flow. That doesn't mean you need to skimp on your rest, or you need to work until you fall over. But you really want to maximize your momentum.

It's essential that over the weekend you treat yourself to good nutrition and adequate rest. If you're eating junk food or trying to get by on just a little bit of sleep, your production is going to suffer. Stay in the flow ... work in the flow as long as you can ... and don't turn the spigot off.

But when it's time to rest, it's time to rest and you need to recognize that.

So what are you going to achieve this weekend? First you're going to pick a topic if you haven't already done so. You may be carrying one around in your mind. Many people already have a topic for one particular reason or another. But if you haven't, that's one thing you're going to do.

You're going to **choose a working title**. It may change somewhere down the road as you get closer to final publication. But you need to have something to begin with that focuses your effort on what you're doing, and a title will help you do just that.

You're going to **research the topic**. One of the things you're going to do this weekend is to outline the topic. (An easier way to put this is you're going to list the steps in logical order.) Writing how-to books often involves specific steps, so you're going to put them in a logical order to help organize your book. Then you're going to create notes after you outline the topic utilizing some initial research. And after you've built your 'skeleton' you're going to put some skin on the bones with additional research.

Then you're going to **create an audio recording** of either your presentation of the information, or of you being interviewed on the topic. That's right. I said you're going to create an audio recording! (Remember, the title of this book is How to Write a Book This Weekend, and that's exactly what you're going to do by creating a recording. As

9

we go further I'll get more into why you're doing it, and the benefit to you of doing it that way.)

When you've got the recording done you'll have the base of your book. You'll have the guts. You'll have what you're going to build everything else on. And once you've got that, you know you have a book. It's going to need some polishing, but that's to be expected. You've got a book, and from there the steps will become much easier.

The final step is to get the recording transcribed, edited, and the finishing touches done. That's likely not going to happen this weekend, unless you've got a super-responsive transcriber and an editor who works around-the-clock. But once you've got the recording done the hard part is out of the way, which is what you should aim to accomplish over the weekend.

Realistically, How Long Will it Take?

To be honest there are a lot of variables to deal with. There's the length required to communicate your information. There are some books that you could communicate everything in 15,000 words; others might take 25,000 to 40,000 or more. As I mentioned previously, information books tend to be on the shorter side. But it's going to be driven by how much information is required to cover the topic you want to present.

Your knowledge level at the outset is going to drive how long it takes. If you're an expert and can speak off-the-cuff at will in deep detail about your subject, it's going to take a lot less time.

For example, I'm an expert on this subject we're discussing today. I have the information and I've done it many times before. I don't have to gather a lot of information, so I can do it a lot speedier than, say, if I went out and decided to do an information book about how to crochet because I know absolutely nothing about that (except I think you use big needles). I'd have to gather a lot of information to fill in what I don't know, which is everything about that particular topic, so it's going to take me much longer.

Your confidence in speaking about your subject matter is going to also impact how long it takes. If you're knowledgeable enough in the area so you can talk off-the-cuff about the topic, you're probably going to have a tremendous amount of confidence that will dramatically shorten how long it takes to complete the work.

Your focus and work ethic are also going to be variables. If it's easy for you to be distracted, and you're not used to working for extended periods of time focused on one particular thing, it's going to take you longer.

We talked earlier about getting in the 'flow' which is what you're trying to achieve, and it takes time to get to that place. It's like creating any type of momentum: There's a certain period of time it takes to build that energy level, but once you're there it's easier to maintain the momentum.

Think of riding a bicycle. There's a lot more energy required in the beginning to get your bicycle up-to-speed; but once it's there it's fairly easy to maintain that momentum. It's the same with maintaining the flow: How good your focus and work ethic are will realistically affect how long it takes.

The speed with which you can research and outline is going to be a big factor in how long it takes. If you're extremely good at research and have done a lot of it before – if you know how to maximize the use of research tools like the Internet, libraries, and those types of resources – you're going to accomplish your task much quicker than, for instance, someone who doesn't really know their way around a search engine.

I could probably do half a book on what all the variables are. But following is a list of some generalized times that might take you to complete these tasks:

- **Picking a Topic**: This is going to take 1+ hours if you don't already have one in mind. The topics of those 50-something books my publishing company produced were researched by someone working with our company or by me. And generally speaking, for us to pick those topics it took us one to two hours of focused time. If you've already got a really good idea you may be done in ten minutes.

- **Preparation**: A big variable to get ready for your weekend that should take 1+ hours.

- **Choosing a Title**: Depending on how good your current communication skills are and how good you are at modeling other titles is another 1+ hour task.

- **Research**: You should allow at least ten hours and probably more. I'd venture to say you'll spend more time researching than all the other elements combined, which is just the nature of writing a book.

  It may take you 5+ hours to do some additional research to add notes or put skin on the skeleton of your outline. Again, this will depend on how well versed you are. If you already have a lot of examples on the tip of your tongue you can instantly recall, then there will be less time involved.

- **Outline and Steps to Your Book**: Organizing your book is probably going to take 2+ hours. As you begin to organize it you're going to see that in some cases you'll want to move ideas around. As you begin to fill in your outline there may be more logical sequences, so it's not something you're going to do quickly.

- **Recording**: It's going to take approximately 1.5 to 2+ hours to create your recording, so you can expect at least 22 hours to execute the critical elements. You'll still have to complete editing and add other elements after that.

As I said before, the biggest part is accomplished when you've recorded the basis to your book. If you're wanting a 15,000 to 20,000 word information how-to book, you're going to be looking at somewhere in the neighborhood of 22 hours, which is why it's perfect for a weekend. You'll be working hard during those 22 hours, and you must be focused 100% on the task at hand.

Don't Allow Distractions to Creep In

Yard work can wait until next weekend. You can go out for dinner and a movie with friends another time. THIS weekend you've got to be FOCUSED!

Still a Doubting Thomas? Don't think you can do it? Afraid you'll fail? The truth is you've got absolutely nothing to lose and everything to gain. Even if you fail, the time spent will prepare you to succeed.

My first website was a big failure. After expecting to make several hundred thousand dollars a year from what I thought was a great idea, I never made one penny. I invested money at a time when I didn't have a whole lot.

And I invested a lot of time and a lot of energy to get zip … nada … nothing. But I was wrong to walk away from that fiasco thinking I had made a big mistake.

I once heard an expression I've never forgotten: "There are no mistakes … only lessons." And I was left with some incredible lessons when I walked away from my first Web failure.

Several years later I'd use those lessons to jumpstart my second website that became profitable in its first 90 days, which is unheard of for start-up businesses. It went on to earn me six figures in its first year, and within a few years was generating seven figures.

Here's a thought: What if it took you twice or four times as long to write a book good enough to sell? Would you give up four weekends to have your own book? If the answer is no, then let me save you time. Close this book <u>now</u> and go on to something else.

But if the answer is a strong and resounding **yes!**, start with the idea that if <u>you</u> lack the belief that you can do it you'll operate on <u>my</u> belief that you can do it because I believe you can. In fact, I <u>know you can write a book this weekend</u>! So let's get started.

(**Attention All Eagle Eyes**: We've had a number of people proof this book before we released it to you, but there is a chance you might spot something that was missed. If you find a typo or other obvious error, please send it to us. And if you're the first one to report it <u>we'll send you a free gift</u>! Send to: corrections@laurenzanapress.com)

CHAPTER 1

Be a Good Scout and Be Prepared

I t will help tremendously if you have a good idea of what topic you want to write about before the week-end starts, as it will allow you to get your subconscious involved by helping you create ideas. I'm sure you've had the experience of standing in the shower and all of a sud-den an idea crystallizes. Or in some other situation, such as driving down the road, an intuitive idea came about as a result of your subconscious being at work.

I might carry an idea for a book around for weeks or even months (and on more than one occasion for years) before I get started. Then by focusing on it from time-to-time I get my subconscious involved. I get that little 'genie' involved and it's going to work 24/7 (but I don't know it's there as it's working in the background in my subconscious).

My 'genie' becomes very efficient at revealing relevant information in the billions of bits of life's data I see every day. It's going to find examples that will make great reading in my book. And it's going to find the stories I want to share with my readers.

I'll be surfing the Web and something will catch my eye. I'll bookmark it because I realize it's relevant to the book. I'll not only bookmark the pages; I'll put links, notes, or relevant paragraphs into a Word document and save it for later. I've created Word documents that I may open four, five or six months later (as I did, by the way, six months ago because I knew I was going to write this book).

I once heard John Maxwell, a prolific bestselling author, describe his system. He reads a lot of magazines, especially while traveling, and when he sees something interesting he'll tear out the article and file it by topic. He has files upon files upon files by topic. When he gets ready to do a book he simply pulls out all the related files, and in doing so he's already completed a big part of writing his book since his research, examples and stories are all in one place.

Anything you can do before the weekend will help as it's going to make you more confident. Even if you only have one hour available during the week there's something you can do. If this is Thursday you can still get a jumpstart, and whatever you do will help you do a better job on the weekend.

It would be a great time before the weekend to read top books on the topic, which you'll need to do in the research phase unless you're already an expert in the subject. And even then, it's still a great idea. If this coming weekend isn't going to work for you, then aim for next weekend or the weekend after. Between now and whatever that target weekend is, locate the top books on your topic and read them.

Make sure you've cleared your calendar for the weekend. You don't want to get some momentum going on Saturday, and then be surprised with a last minute must attend event or chore you overlooked. You really want to do everything you can to be focused on one thing and get in the flow of doing that: And that is <u>writing your book this weekend</u>!

CHAPTER 2

Pick a Niche and a Topic

I could easily devote one or more books to the subject of picking a topic. Although that's not the focus of this book, let's spend a few minutes talking about its importance and an overview of how to do it.

It'll make your task many times simpler, and more likely to succeed, if you have some knowledge in the area. Why? Well, you're going to understand the language. Every area of life, whether it's occupation or hobby, has its own 'language.' For instance, if you're around a bunch of fishermen and you have no experience or knowledge of fishing, you could get lost in their conversation. Their 'language' would include words you don't understand, but have very specific meaning to the fishermen since they understand their own 'language.'

Having some knowledge in the area and understanding the language is going to make it a lot easier for you to put your book together. In fact, everyone has areas of interest, and that's where I try to point people for their very first book as it's important to get that first one under your belt.

As you become more accomplished in this particular strategy, you can expand to areas where you don't have any knowledge. And if you don't have any knowledge and you still want to proceed, not to worry. You can become an expert quicker than you think. Maybe not by this weekend, but many times more rapidly thanks to the Internet.

In his classic work, <u>Lead the Field</u>, Earl Nightingale said over 50 years ago that in "…five years or less you can become a true expert in your field. And it's the experts who write their own tickets in life."

Thanks to modern technology that time has shrunk to a year or less to become a national expert. **A year or less!** In fact, I went from being completely unknown in the personal development field to becoming an <u>internationally</u> known expert in goal-setting in about <u>18 months</u>! The first time I was paid to speak I commanded $7,500 plus expenses for just over an hour's worth of speaking. I made half as much money that day as I had made the entire year of 1997!

Stupendous speaking fees are the motivation for many people wanting to write a book. Some celebrities make it on the speaking circuit without having written a book; but it is the rare non-celebrity who does so since a successful book adds almost instant authority and credibility.

Once again, if this is your first book pick a topic and a niche you have some knowledge in. If you have little or no

knowledge, pick one you have a strong desire ᴦᴄ
fluent in. It will make book writing easier, and will be accompanied by many serendipities.

Amazon is the obvious first step. Go to the Search box
and change the department to Kindle Store; then start
typing keywords related to your topic. A menu under the
Search box will drop down, and you'll see ten suggestions
made by Amazon based on what you typed – a great
indication of what people are searching for under those
particular keywords, and they're going to be listed in the
order of their popularity.

A cool piece of new software that actually automates
that process as well as giving you the current trending
information from Google Trends can be found at http://
GetFreshKey.com. It's only $20 right now (but as word
gets out I would expect demand might take the price up),
and it turns what could be hours of work into seconds.

Can you imagine an author in the years before the
Internet needing to do the kind of research we're talking
about? Where would they have gone to get that? They
probably ended up in a library with thousands of physical
volumes to go through.

But now you can do that in a matter of minutes, and
certainly much quicker just by going to one website where
you can get sales data, the rankings of the books, and how
popular a particular title or topic is. You can click on the
topics at Amazon and it will list the number of books it
has in that topic just above the results, which is incredible
pre-planning research available at your fingertips.

FreshKey

FRESHKEY

green smoothies

🔍 Get Keywords

🔁 Get Keywords

✖ Stop Search

⦿ Google

● Amazon

⦿ Spin Text

Rank	Service	Keywords	Trend
1	Amazon	green smoothies	
2	Amazon	green smoothies diet	
3	Amazon	green smoothies for weight loss	
4	Amazon	green smoothies recipes	
5	Amazon	green smoothies for beginners	
6	Amazon	green smoothies book	
7	Amazon	green smoothies diet the natural program for extraordinary health	
8	Amazon	green smoothies for dummies	
9	Amazon	green smoothies for life	
10	Amazon	green smoothies and juices	
1	Amazon	green smoothies book	
1	Amazon	green smoothies cancer	
2	Amazon	green smoothies cookbook	
1	Amazon	green smoothies diet	
2	Amazon	green smoothies diet the natural program for extraordinary health	
1	Amazon	green smoothies for weight loss	
2	Amazon	green smoothies for beginners	
3	Amazon	green smoothies for dummies	
4	Amazon	green smoothies for life	
5	Amazon	green smoothies for every season	

Showing 25 results

📋 Copy To Clipboard   ⤓ Export To File   ⊿ View Trend

GetFreshKey.com

I've told people that at times it felt like my eyes were literally bleeding from the time I've spent researching information on Amazon. It's such a wealth of data that I find myself drilling down and drilling down and drilling down. I come away with a great deal of statistics that help me understand, number one, what the marketplace is looking for. And number two, shows me people who are already successful in that marketplace.

Now don't be concerned if you've come up with a topic and there are already successful authors in that genre at Amazon; in fact, you should expect there will be. I would be very concerned if I came up with a topic and there weren't already some successful books, because that might be a definite indicator there's not a lot of interest in that topic.

Don't worry that there are other books with information either similar to or the same as what you're attempting to produce. When people buy information they don't buy just one book. If you went to college and majored in history, you wouldn't go all the way through your college career with just one history book; you'd buy and study multiple books in order to become knowledgeable in that field. And that's the way people buy information books today.

When you go on Amazon and look at a book, it will suggest other books based on what other people buy. For instance, if people pull up my goal-setting book, one of the other books they buy is a goal-setting book by my friend

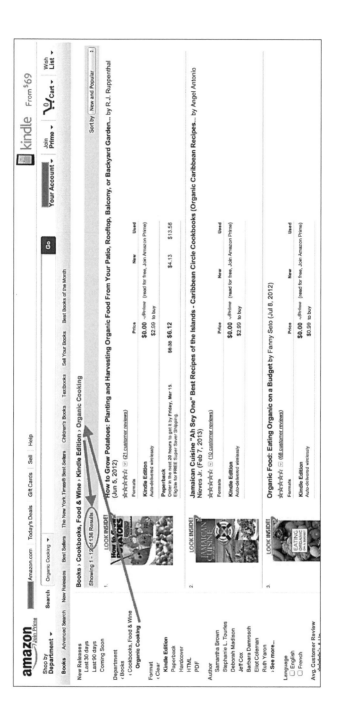

amazon
Join Prime

Shop by Department ▾ | Search | Your Account ▾ | Join Prime ▾ | Cart ▾ | Wish List ▾

Amazon.com | Today's Deals | Gift Cards | Sell | Help

Books | Advanced Search | New Releases | Best Sellers | The New York Times® Best Sellers | Children's Books | Textbooks | Sell Your Books | Best Books of the Month

New Releases
Last 30 days
Last 90 days
Coming Soon

Department
‹ Books
‹ Cookbooks, Food & Wine
Organic Cooking

Format
‹ Clear
Kindle Edition
Paperback
Hardcover
HTML
PDF

Author
Samantha Brown
Stephanie L. Tourles
Deborah Madison
Jeff Cox
Barbara Damrosch
Eliot Coleman
Ruth Yaron
› See more...

Language
☐ English
☐ French

Avg. Customer Review

Organic Cooking ▾ | Go

Books › Cookbooks, Food & Wine › Kindle Edition › Organic Cooking

Showing 1 - 12 of 136 Results

Sort by New and Popular ▾

1. How to Grow Potatoes: Planting and Harvesting Organic Food From Your Patio, Rooftop, Balcony, or Backyard Garden... by R.J. Ruppenthal (Jun 5, 2012)
★★★★☆ ▷ (21 customer reviews)

Formats	Price	New	Used
Kindle Edition Auto-delivered wirelessly	$0.00 ✓Prime (read for free, Join Amazon Prime)		
	$2.99 to buy		
Paperback Order in the next 20 hours to get it by Friday, Mar 15. Eligible for FREE Super Saver Shipping.	$6.38 $6.12	$4.13	$13.58

2. Jamaican Cuisine "Ah Sey One" Best Recipes of the Islands - Caribbean Circle Cookbooks (Organic Caribbean Recipes... by Angel Antonio Nieves Jr. (Feb 7, 2013)
★★★★☆ ▷ (10 customer reviews)

Formats	Price	New	Used
Kindle Edition Auto-delivered wirelessly	$0.00 ✓Prime (read for free, Join Amazon Prime)		
	$2.99 to buy		

3. Organic Food: Eating Organic on a Budget by Fanny Seto (Jul 8, 2012)
★★★★☆ ▷ (68 customer reviews)

Formats	Price	New	Used
Kindle Edition Auto-delivered wirelessly	$0.00 ✓Prime (read for free, Join Amazon Prime)		
	$0.99 to buy		

LOOK INSIDE!

LOOK INSIDE!

LOOK INSIDE!

Craig Ballantyne and vice versa. I'm not upset that they'll buy Craig's book (as long as they buy mine). And I know Craig's not upset that they bought my book (as long as they buy his as well). When people are looking for a solution to one of their problems they'll often buy multiple books in order to get that information.

Google is the next obvious place as it's a diamond mine for book ideas. You can find the data on highly searched keywords by using the Adwords keyword tool. Google Trends shows you the increase or decline in interest for popular search terms, so you're going to see real-time what is or isn't trending on Google.

You can set up Google alerts to notify you any time Google has anything new on your topic. If you're not quite ready to get underway with your book, set up some Google alerts now and it will start feeding you occurrences. When it indexes something new – whether it's a Web or a news item – it will send you an alert, and you can see if it's something you want to file for later use.

After you've written your book set up Google alerts for your name and a separate one for the title of your book, which can help you identify potential audiences for the ongoing promotion of your work.

www.CBtrends.com is another great tool for determining the most popular products on ClickBank, where eBooks sometimes sell for as much as $97. And there are many eBooks there in the range of $27 to $37 (which is pretty expensive by Amazon's standards for an eBook). If someone is willing to spend that kind of money for that kind of information, it probably shows a pretty strong interest in that area. And CBtrends helps you see which topic areas are the best sellers.

If Google is a diamond mine for eBook ideas, then Yahoo Answers is a goldmine as it allows you to see in real-time the real life topics people are searching for.

One of the earliest business maxims I heard was "to be successful, find a need and fill it." Instead of coming up with a book you think is a great idea, why not come up with an idea assisted by what the marketplace tells you is something people are looking for?

At Yahoo Answers you can see the kinds of questions people are asking in a particular topic area, whether it be weight loss, health, education – any kind of field at all. It's amazing the types of questions you'll see. Some are silly and some are almost ignorant, but you'll find a wealth of information on Yahoo Answers. But the most important thing you'll find is a source of really good topics people need information on.

We're just getting started with places to go: YouTube, blogs, forums and social media are also endless wells of ideas. YouTube has a special category of how-to videos, and you can see the types that are most popular. And popularity is driven by what? The crowd clicks on the video and watches it, so it's driven by views. YouTube is another great source of data that's not guesswork; it's real information you can make a decision on.

You may come up with a valid excuse for not creating your book (though I'm at a loss to think of one). But I can assure you that not being able to come up with an idea isn't valid as there are just too many places to find them. Here are some tips:

Aim for Evergreen Books

What do I mean by 'evergreen books'? An evergreen book is going to be good this month, six months, two years and ten years from now because the information doesn't expire, or it may expire way into the future.

If I were doing a book about the upcoming Olympics I could perhaps sell that book to everyone who was interested in who the participants might be, or other relevant information and statistics about the Olympics. But what's going to happen once the Olympics have come and gone? There's going to be very few buyers for my book, so that is not an evergreen book.

A book about a current hot news story or celebrity is probably not an evergreen book. As time goes on the shelf life will decline tremendously.

We published a book by my friend, Ron White, <u>How to Improve Your Memory in 30 Days</u>. Will that information be just as useful 20, 30, 50 years from now? Absolutely! Therefore, it qualifies as an <u>evergreen</u> book. Evergreen books have the magic of paying residual income well into the future, which is what attracted me to information and how-to books. And what attracted me to publishing books was the ability to create residual evergreen income.

I'd like to encourage you to look at other evergreen books, and Dale Carnegie is a great example. You may have heard of him in any number of ways, but in 1936 he wrote a bestselling book called <u>How to Win Friends and Influence People</u>, which in 1936 was a very important topic. And every year since it's continued to be an important topic as witnessed by the fact it's been on the bestseller list since 1936. Dale died in 1955, but it's <u>still</u> a bestseller and earning tens of thousands of dollars a year in royalties. Why? No matter the age, people will always be interested in attracting friends and being able to influence others.

Still don't have any ideas?

Look at the Main Things People Spend Money On

People are always looking for good information about their appearance, their health, their love life, their hobbies. And these are the kinds of things people will spend money on to get information they don't currently have.

Be Alert to Popular
Infomercials

Seeing them on a regular basis means the advertiser is making money. It also means it's a potential topic for an information book, because it proves people will spend money for that kind of information.

The topics of offers you get in the mail tell you about your interest. (As I pointed out earlier, your interest can help you find a topic since you're already familiar with the language.) You're getting particular offers because the mailers have identified that's probably an interest from your prior purchasing habits.

But it also tells you about what's selling right now. Marketers spend billions of dollars every year to mail offers to the public, and they're not going to be mailing the offers consistently – like the infomercial producer – if they're not returning a steady source of income. If the mailers weren't working they'd give up and spend their money elsewhere. But they are working, and that's a great source of new ideas for a book.

CHAPTER 3

Choose a Working Title

I t may not be your final title, but having something to begin with helps focus your thoughts, activity, and all your effort. This step is much like choosing a topic (and easily the subject of an entire book itself), and is probably the <u>single-most</u> important thing you'll do in writing your book. Even though it's outside the focus of this book, let's spend a few minutes on choosing the best title.

Back in the early part of the 20th century a Russian immigrant named E. Haldeman-Julius came up with the idea of publishing what he called the "Little Blue Books." They were indeed small books as they were 4" x 6" and about 60 pages long – a quick reading a blue-collar worker could stick in his pocket or lunchbox, or a lady could stick in her purse. Many times it was information; sometimes it was a reprint of old classic public domain works.

At significant expense Haldeman-Julius printed these books and developed a strategy to help sell them. He'd list only the title of the books he had, the price of the books, and a line for the buyer to fill in the quantity. Typically the order form would be an 8" x 11" page with all the titles listed. He didn't include any descriptions; all the buyer had to make a decision on was the title of a particular book.

At the end of the year Julius would analyze his sales. If any book had sold less than 10,000 copies, he'd change the title and offer it in the coming year under the new title. Then he'd do the same process as he had before, offering them for sale with nothing more to go on except the title.

What Julius did resulted in one of the greatest research tools in understanding what titles worked and what motivates people to buy, because that's all they had to make a decision on at that time. That, my friend, is the *power* of a good title. E. Haldeman Julius understood that a title alone could be the deciding factor in whether someone would make a purchase, and he proved that year after year after year.

If you want to get a great understanding of the "psychology" of a good title, Amazon and other booksellers sell Haldeman-Julius' book on the subject called <u>The First Hundred Million</u>. The title, of course, referred to how he sold his first hundred million books and it's fascinating.

Today's world, where there are many other things to go along with a title (i.e., on Amazon where you can have a description, a cover and even a sample of the book), is a bit different from Haldeman-Julius's day. But what isn't different is the title is the <u>most important thing</u> in helping someone decide whether or not they want to purchase a book.

Your title is essentially a headline, like you might find in sales material that someone mails you, or the big bold words at the top of a magazine ad. Headlines and titles are in many ways interchangeable. And in fact, many people who write good titles use the same formulas good headline writers use to come up with great headlines.

My book, <u>How I Created a Six-Figure Income Giving Away a Dead Guy's Book</u>, was adapted from some bestselling headlines. You can study the most effective headlines, and from those you can create titles as powerful as the headlines themselves.

Another tool to use is the Keywords Questions tab at www.freekeywords.wordtracker.com/keyword-questions. This will show you the actual input of questions people put into search engines when trying to find information.

For example, if you're trying to appeal to a particular audience and you can write a title that answers the question they're asking while looking for that information, would they be more or less likely to buy your book? (You know the answer to that one without me saying it.)

When you go to the www.freekeywords.wordtracker website, you'll notice how many questions are how-to questions. You'll also notice how many books begin with or include the words "how to," because 'how to' is still one of the very best headline formulas ever. And I see no time in the future when it won't be.

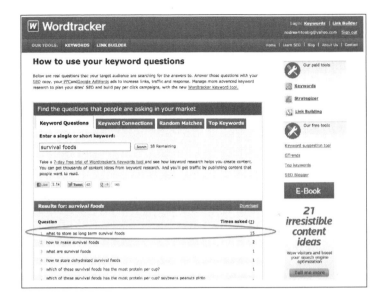

I previously used the example of Ron White's ***How to Improve Your Memory in Just 30 Days***. The title of this book is ***How to*** Write a Book This Weekend, Even if You Flunked English Like I Did.

As I previously mentioned, one of the biggest books of all time is ***How to*** Win Friends and Influence People. The words "how to" are still popular and get results, or you wouldn't see them in so many titles.

The alternate is "How I." For example, Frank Bettger wrote a bestselling book, ***How I*** Raised Myself From Failure to Success in Selling. If you're in sales, does that sound like information you'd be interested in? Of course it does, especially if you haven't been selling too much lately.

And again my book, ***How I*** Created a Six-Figure Income Giving Away a Dead Guy's Book.

Good titles usually contain a promise or an expected benefit. Notice the title of this book: *How to* Write a Book This Weekend Even if You Flunked English Like I Did. What's the promise and/or the expected benefit?

First, you'd expect that you're going to be able to write a book this weekend. Second, you'd expect that you don't have to be the sharpest Crayon in the box, and you can succeed even if you're not a polished writer. So those are benefits the person who might look at this title could expect.

How to Win Friends and Influence People. All human beings want to have friends. They want those friends to respect them, and be able to influence people to do things they'd like for them to do or to help them in some way. Those are HUGE benefits, HUGE promises, which is why such books are so popular.

Today Amazon, Apple and other online bookstores are very keyword sensitive. And that means having at least one of your major keywords included in the title is going to help when people search for your book. In fact, we've put up books at Apple with no other promotion than the title containing some strong keywords, and those books have been ranked in the top five based on the strength of those keywords. So keep that in mind while you're thinking of a title.

One word of caution: Amazon will yank your book down and possibly close your account if you're guilty of keyword-stuffing your title. You've probably seen the books I'm talking about: the titles seem to go on forever but don't often make a lot of sense.

With just a little study it's easy to see that the author is trying to use multiple major keywords. The most I've ever been able to fit into a title where its still sensible sounding is two.

Want some ideas to help with your title selection?

You Can Download 405 Title Ideas from TitleIdeas.com

CHAPTER 4

Researching The Topic

You may have done this in your getting prepared stage. But if you haven't, you'll want to read or at least skim through top books about your topic, which is critical to understanding the available knowledge about your particular topic.

Knowing what other people are writing will give you guidance in terms of the kind of information the marketplace is looking for, as long you're reading the top books in your niche. Reading literature that already exists and making notes as you go is one of the biggest components of putting your book together.

You can't copy and paste long passages or chapters from someone else's work as it's a violation of copyright laws. However, you can and should "synthesize" that information. What does 'synthesize' mean? Reading the material, applying your thinking processes, and then putting the resulting product in your own words is 'synthesizing' the information. If you take the top three books and read their coverage on a particular topic, you can put that into your own words and thoughts. You're *synthesizing* that information, and you're not infringing on someone else's copyright.

You can quote from other works as long as you use a reasonable passage. This book isn't designed to give legal advice; however, there are many Internet articles about the legal term "fair use" that describes what you can use and how you can use it. But understand that when you quote from someone's work it's important to give credit to the source.

If a story or fact sounds too good to be true, stop and verify it. Don't assume that since it's in writing that it's true. For instance, I've often heard a story about goal-setting (since that's a field I'm an expert in I'm going to be very sensitive to such a story since it would add to my repertoire) utilizing Yale University (and sometimes Harvard) students.

As the story goes, they tracked 100 students for 20 years after they graduated, and studied where the students ended up income and success-wise. To make the long story short, 3% of the class had written goals in the beginning and ended up being successful (the obvious point being if you write down your goals you'll be successful. Well, we know from other studies and other instances that fact is indeed true: Written goals are very powerful in achievement.)

However, the Yale/Harvard study is false – it never happened. It's an urban legend and has been repeated thousands of times, sometimes by the biggest names in personal development. In fact, you'll find thousands of references to it on the Web, but it's not true.

So <u>verify</u>! If something you read sounds a little out of the ordinary or too good to be true, don't doubt that it's true. But verify it before you repeat it, or use it as an example.

If you've got the budget you can save the time reading the best books in the field by buying a book summary, which will give you the key points of the literature. If no summary is available you can hire freelancers to read and summarize the book, and put the summary into an outline form (which will help you later with your exercise).

It's also important early on to identify primary keywords that relate to your book. Nowadays in the world of Google and Internet search, keywords are what it's all about. The time you spend doing this will be some of the best quality time if you do it right. You'll use keywords from the beginning of your research and throughout the promotion of your book.

If you don't already know, a 'keyword' is simply one or more words people use to search for information. For example, if they're searching for footwear, "brown shoes" might be put into a search engine (the key words being "brown shoes"). Typically it's one or more words used to search for information in a particular area.

You can go to www.smashwords.com, and the books in your area of interest are listed by topic. You can click on a topic, or put in a general keyword for your book like "goal-setting." Pulling up the sales page on that book at Smashwords will show you the tags associated with that book (a great source of keywords as it helps you understand what people might use to search for that book. And if your book is in a similar area it would ideally be used to search for your book as well.)

Then you'll compile a list of the tags and go to the Keywords Ideas tool at www.adwords.google.com. You'll take all the tags you found – you'll want as many as you possibly can – and paste them in the Search box at the keywords tool at www.adwords.google.com and click Search.

Google will then take those tags and generate a number of ideas on different keywords. You're probably going to end up with hundreds, if not thousands, of suggestions. You'll obviously look for keywords that are searched the most, so you'll sort by volume of searches and will look at those from the top down. You can download the entire list as a CSV (Comma Separated Value) file, and open it in a spreadsheet which will help you manipulate and manage the data Google provides.

Then you're going to filter out the 20 best. (Some of Google's keyword ideas won't make any sense at all, which is part of the automation and dealing with a massive machine like Google. But you're going to be able to come up with the 20 best based on volume and relevance.)

Then you're going to take those 20 best keywords, go to

Amazon, and enter each of them in the Search box where it will show you additional information in the drop-down menu of ten titles or search keywords associated with what you just entered. This will help you look at some additional keywords. And it's also going to help you pull up books in your topic area so you can then begin to drill down and learn more about how those keywords generate a particular return of a list of books.

You're then going to open a blank spreadsheet and save the best ten keywords that came from your exercise at Amazon (you'll find many uses for these ten keywords as you move forward).

www.EzineArticles.com is probably the best and oldest source for articles people have written on a myriad of topics, and it's a great place for researching your topic. Here's a code you can enter into a Google search box that will pull up all the articles with your preferred keywords at EzineArticles:

site:ezinearticles.com "your keywords go here" "Viewed 10...4999 times." "Submitted On * *, 2012"

Replace your keywords within the quotes (don't delete the quotes). "10" currently represents the lowest viewed, and "4999" the maximum views. You can substitute your own numbers for these.

The year submitted is set to 2012, which can be changed as well to any year you want.

After you've made the substitutions above, copy and paste this entire code into a Google search box. If you don't get any results, change the variables (keyword, views, or year) and try again.

Some people may say the research step should come after the outline step. But how do you know what the key parts of your outline are if you haven't done any research? That's why you'll do significant research before you start to outline your book. Besides, you're not done with research when you finish this step (as you'll see in a minute).

CHAPTER 5

Outline The Topic, or List The Steps In Logical Order

O ne thing I like about how-to and information books is they typically follow a logical sequence of some type of steps, which makes it very easy to organize your book since a natural sequence is already in place. But regardless of whether there is a natural sequence or you need to create a certain sequence, you'll want to gather all your material together. If it's physical material, you'll want to shuffle the pages in a loosely organized fashion. Or you can use software (I use a mind map from www.mindjet.com) to create a mind map of your information.

You'll want to look at your outline you're going to create as your Table of Contents. Open the front of any book to the Table of Contents, and you'll see that as a logical sequence in an information or how-to book since it steps you through the information in a certain order.

When you're creating an outline you're establishing

your Table of Contents. Each main point or step is a chapter in your book; and the sub-points, or the parts to each step, are subchapters.

The great personal development speaker, Zig Ziglar, used to tell audiences the way he was instructed to speak was to tell them what you're going to tell them … tell them … and then tell them what you told them. Which is a great illustration of how you should make a presentation of any kind, whether it's speaking or writing. Every presentation should have a beginning (you tell them what you're going to tell them); a middle (now you tell them); and an end (you tell them what you told them, or a summary that applies to the book overall and to each chapter).

If you can put together 10 to 12 chapters, and within each chapter 10 to 12 key points, you're going to have the basis of your book. I've seen it done with fewer chapters and fewer key points, but aim for those as a good beginning point.

You'll add to that an Introduction and a Conclusion, and you're ready to go. Sometimes instead of a summary or a Conclusion I want to have a call-to-action since I want them to take the next step. I want the reader having read my information to go on to what's next, and I'll invite them to that very same conclusion.

In putting together your outline you'll start with the big questions to answer. That's why research tools like Yahoo Answers are so valuable as you can find out what those big questions are. Then arranging those big questions helps you form some or all of your chapters. You can never go wrong with the dependable formula W5H: who, what, when, where, how, and why. By creating your questions from that formula, you'll likely have answered the major questions your readers have on a particular topic.

W5H, by the way, is a handy tool to use in any problem-solving situation. Though I had heard it referred to many times, I'd never taken the time to actively use it. Once I did I felt like Superman as it forces your conscious and subconscious mind to deliver some ideas. When you're trying to solve problems, the more ideas you have the better.

Don't worry if your outline doesn't follow the rules you learned in school. Remember, I flunked English and none of my outlines would pass muster. Again, it's not meant to be a formal outline but more of a Table of Contents. As long as it helps you arrange your information in an orderly, logical way, it's achieving its purpose.

Before you proceed, you might pass along your Table of Contents to someone who has some knowledge of your topic and ask them "Is this a logical sequence?" Or it might be someone in your target market who's looking for the kind of information you'll be providing. Ask them, "Did I leave anything out? Is there something that doesn't need to be there?" This then will become the skeleton of what you're going to put a 'skin' on as you move forward.

CHAPTER 6

Create Notes With Additional Research Time

T his is where your outline comes to life. You're going to be attaching notes to each of the points of your outline, just as you'd do if you were to present this information in front of an audience (a great analogy to keep in the forefront of your mind if you've made presentations before. You're going to use the same skills you used previously to prepare a presentation.)

What are the key stories or examples that help make the point? Stories – as long they're interesting, relevant, non-rambling and fairly succinct – are time-honored ways to communicate your points.

Without getting religious here, I'd like to point out that in the New Testament most of the words Jesus spoke involved some type of story or allegory. Jesus knew the easiest way to teach others was through the use of a story. And the reason for that is if you go back to your childhood, that's the way you were taught the first things in life.

People read and told stories to you, which was one of your first forms of learning. And for your entire life it's been a tool that allowed you to understand bigger concepts in a way that made them easily assimilated. (Did you recognize that I just made a key point by using a story?)

This then is the last step before creating a recording of your work. At this point you may see some areas of your outline that are sparser than others, and some areas may have too much information in them. If you have the time to fill in the sparse areas, do so. If you don't, don't sweat it as you can fill them in during the editing phase.

Your main purpose is to record the information you have so you can have something on paper to work with. I work backwards to determine how much time I have to finish my additional research. If I want to finish at 6:00 p.m. on Sunday evening, and my anticipated recording time is two hours, I'm going to stop my research around 2:00 p.m. so I can have at least an hour or so to review my outline and notes, and 30 minutes to grab a bite to eat and relax before starting my recording. (Be sure to eat protein and vegetables, and don't indulge too much or you'll be too drowsy.)

Using this example I'm going to work like a maniac until 3:30 and then it's break time. If I have to fill spots in later on, so be it. My goal is to send the recording to my transcriptionist Sunday night, and I WILL make my goal.

CHAPTER 7

Create an Audio Recording

You understand the frustration if you've ever sat down to write and experienced writer's block. You've probably heard writer after writer explain that all writers have writer's block, and the way out of that is simply to write.

That's certainly one solution, but I found an easier solution that works for me. For some people, speaking their book is easier than writing it. Think about it: People spend a lot more time of their day speaking than they do writing, and most are far more comfortable with speaking than they are with writing.

I find it a lot easier to write if the pump is already primed. In other words, if there are already productive words on the page, it's easier for me to get into the flow. I find a place to jump in, and it seems easier at that point for the written word to come to me. And that's what this exercise is going to do. We're going to get the basic words of your book on paper without writing them!

Let me ask you a question: If one of your friends asked

you to tell them about your favorite hobby, could you give them an earful? Would they eventually have to tell you to shut up because in your enthusisasm to share the information you'd ramble on and on?

Well, that's what you're going to be doing. You're going to be presenting your outline and notes this weekend as if you're talking to that friend and unloading all you know about your topic.

Or you can imagine you're practicing to give the presentation in front of a group. You're literally going to be "speaking your book into existence." Don't believe this method will work? Brian Tracy, who's had more than 50 books published in 38 languages (a number of which have been bestsellers) says, "When I began writing I converted my audio programs, each of which had 12 parts, into a series of 12-chapter books." Think that excludes you because you don't have an audio program?

Listen to what else he says: "Dictating your book is one of the most powerful exercises I have ever discovered, and dramatically increases the speed at which you create your initial manuscript. When you dictate you're forced to write in a conversational tone of voice. This adds warmth to your material, and makes it easier and more enjoyable to read for the reader."

I agree with Brian. In fact, most of the feedback I get about my books always says something about my conversational tone. My readers always feel as though I'm speaking to them, and that's exactly what I want to achieve. This method has worked for Brian Tracy, me, and thousan others, and it <u>will</u> work for you!

I use Audacity software for Mac, which is free, and a Logitech USB headset. But any kind of microphone is fine, even the one in your computer. It doesn't have to be a studio quality recording, but it needs to be clear enough for a transcriber to accurately transcribe. I speak at about 175 wpm, so an hour-and-a-half to two hours of recording gives me approximately 15,000 to 20,000 words which, as I said earlier, in most cases is plenty of words for an information book.

If you find it hard to give a presentation to no one, an alternative strategy is to have someone interview you, which works easier for some people. In that case you'd take the chapters, and the 10 to 12 points you're making in each chapter, and turn each of them into a question. Then you'd have a friend or anyone you're comfortable with interview you in person or over the phone. Of course, you'll want to record the interview.

Tell the interviewer that it's okay to probe if they're not clear about one of your answers. Or if your answer is sparse, tell them it's okay to do a follow-up. Your goal is to get as much as you can down on paper, and that's going to start with getting as much as you can in your recording.

Another alternative is doing a presentation in front of a group. Presenting to groups – whether it's at work or in the community – is another great way to create an audio recording. Several of my books have come from transcriptions of presentations I gave to an audience in much the same way Brian Tracy created his. I've told people to never speak in front of any group without recording it as you never know what that content can be used. That strategy has served me very, very well. I've created many articles and books from presentations where I had no intention at the time for them to end up as an article or a book.

Which goes to my point I made earlier: I really like doing things once and not having to repeat them. And being able to repurpose content is something that fits that style.

The bottom line is you don't have to be a professional speaker to speak your book into existence. You talk every day, right? So just talk and refer to your notes to keep you on track while you record. Don't worry if you ramble. Don't worry if you stumble – it's all going to be edited anyway. The main thing is to record everything you have to say on the topic (progressing in the order of your outline), and it'll be cleaned up later.

CHAPTER 8

Have The Recording Transcribed

T his is by far the easiest task you'll have while writing your book. Some people use voice recognition software that converts the spoken word to the written word. An example is Dragon Naturally Speaking. (I haven't used that software recently, so I can't comment on its effectiveness. But I can say that I prefer using a human transcriptionist as there's less clean-up to do.) You can find transcriptionists all over the Web at sites like www.elance.com and www.odesk.com. Some charge by the hour and others by the minutes of recording.

I've had extremely good luck in this area as I've only used two transcriptionists during my ten years of doing this, and they're both gems. (The contact information for Mary Jo can be found on the Resources page at the end of the book.)

Expect to pay somewhere between $1.00 to $1.50 per minute of recording. I've had turnaround in as little as 24 hours, but I normally allow for about a week. As with most things, you can pay a reasonable rush charge if you want it sooner.

Deliver the transcriptionist an MP3 audio file of the recording (you can easily create the MP3 with the software we discussed in the previous chapter).

As you're recording, don't worry if you make a mistake. Just back up to where the last good recording ended, start over from that point, and continue on. The transcriptionist and editing will eliminate that information, so you don't need to edit the recording.

If you need to take a break, you can pause the recording and come back to it picking up where you left off.

(At the end of this book is some very helpful information about recording your book. It's written by the transcriptionist I mentioned above – Mary Jo – so you're getting it straight from the horse's mouth.)

CHAPTER 9

Edit The Transcription

E diting the transcription is one of the more difficult parts, because finding a reliable, capable editor can be a challenge. There are many who claim themselves to be 'editors,' but are really just glorified proofreaders.

Good editors aren't just skilled at spotting typos and correcting grammar; they have the skill for allowing the author's style and personality to shine through while ensuring the flow and focus enhances the reader's experience. This may mean moving parts around, and removing or even rewriting some sections.

My track record at www.elance.com is about 50%. In other words, half the time I've found someone that's acceptable or good; the other half has been a miserable failure. However, this is where I employ one of my tricks, which is to hire multiple editors and give them each a chapter to edit. I pay them all for the chapters, and then give the final job to the one who submitted the best editing. It costs me a little more money and takes a little more time, but I'm almost never disappointed or frustrated. (By the way, I use this same trick any time I hire freelancers. I break the job into small representative pieces; outsource three or more pieces; and give the big job to the winner.)

(Mary Jo Stresky has provided our editing for the last several books I've done, and her contact information is on the Resources page. Use it only if you promise not to maximize her time so she doesn't have any time left for me!)

Once you've found a freelancer who does good work, build a relationship with them and send them work and referrals any time you can. The extra effort will come back to you one hundred-fold or more.

One of my transcriptionists has been with me for ten years. My graphic designer, who's done every one of my book covers, has been with me for more than ten years. Not only do they bring stability to my operation, but I think I get better prioritized service and performance than if I were a one-time or infrequent client.

CHAPTER 10

The Finishing Touches

W hen the first edit is done you're not through, but you're substantially down the road and getting closer to finishing your book. Going through the book at this point you'll need to ask yourself **is the book in your "voice"**? In other words, I've had editors who changed the words so much that it no longer sounded like my book.

If you're going to build an audience (and I hope your goal is to do just that, and hopefully this will include multiple books) you'll need to create a relationship with that audience. And part of that is speaking to them in a voice they'll recognize as yours.

The second thing you'll be doing as you go through your book is you'll want to **add more details, facts or stories**. Going through the sparse parts (where the first time through you didn't have a lot of details or facts) is a great place to insert a story to make the point.

Do a second editing yourself. You'll want to go through the book word-by-word, inserting/deleting/

changing words that came back from the first editing. And then you'll want to send it out for a final editing. You can go through this process innumerable times – seven, eight edits or more. But generally speaking I'm pretty satisfied after my first edit and then a final edit.

This would be a good time to **add a quote at the beginning of each chapter** if it applies to your particular book. If you're going to do a book on vertical gardening, it's not necessary to have a quote at the beginning of each chapter as it's probably not relevant to that particular type of book. But in the personal development field a quote certainly helps to enhance the readers' experience as it opens their mind and prepares them for what they're about to read.

Another thing that can be very helpful is to **add an action or to-do list at the end of each chapter**, which adds value to the readers' experience. They've been given the information as to what they should do and how to do it, and now they're given the marching orders for doing it. Plus, the reader gets more value from the book, which will definitely increase your readership loyalty over time.

Use multiple proofreaders as you're finalizing your book. I've seen some of the very best proofreaders miss what would appear to be some very obvious errors – that's just human nature – so you can never have too many proofreaders during a final editing.

After our multiple proofreaders are done, we're still not through. A powerful strategy we use is "crowd sourcing" corrections, which is extremely helpful for a number

of reasons. (At the end of the Introduction to
you'll see an invitation to submit any correctioı
spots; in return we send them a small gift. We've used that
strategy for quite some time, and it's amazing the input
we get.)

Number one, many people are surprised we're asking
for the information and inviting to be told about our
mistakes. Number two, it allows us to establish commu-
nications with our readers. And number three, it uncovers
some really important errors that might have been missed
by editors and proofreaders; therefore, it's a wonderful
process you probably should consider.

Individual and Optional
Pages

Title and Publishing:

Don't forget about adding these pages to your book
as you begin to finalize it. Of course, you have to have a
title page, which is just as it says: it's going to have the title
across the top of the page in a good size type. Underneath
that as you drop down it's going to have the author's name.

Then at the bottom of the page it might be typical to
have the name of the publishing company (at the front
of this book we use a piece of art in addition to the name
that represents a castle in the town of Laurenzana, which
is where my family originated from. And since it's called

"Laurenzana Press," I felt the castle was appropriate and a kind of trademark or logo to identify our business.)

Copyright:

If you look at dozens of copyright pages you'll see that most all of them have a similar format, and they're going to contain the information about the copyright.

One of the things about this whole process – just like any key to success – is learning a modeling process called the "Greek formula for success" (because you can go back to ancient Greeks to see how they used it in achievement). If you find someone doing what you want to do, study in detail what they did, and repeat their steps you'll and achieve the same success. This is called "modeling," and the same process applies when you're writing a book.

Remember, this book is not focused on things of a legal nature, so I would suggest you familiarize yourself with basic copyright laws. But it's enough to say that you do want to have a copyright page in your book, and there are plenty out there on which to model yours.

Table of Contents:

You'll want to have a Table of Contents page, which basically you've already produced because you've written your outline or your steps. The Table of Contents page could include some of the subchapters as well.

Requesting Reviews:

One of the most important things about selling books online is the reviews, so you'll want to have a page dedicated to requesting reviews. Unfortunately, it seems dissatisfied readers are more likely to give you a bad review than people satisfied with your book giving you a good review. For some reason people who are satisfied are less likely to speak up, but bad reviewers seem to have no problem at all posting a disgruntled review.

You should request that readers post their feedback as a review. Doing it in a pleasant way can encourage someone who enjoyed your book but wasn't intending on writing a review to do so.

Sources (or References):

An optional page would include the sources you used. The type of book you're producing will determine whether or not this is important. For instance, if you're producing a book about something of a health nature and the research was from significant clinical information and testing, you'd probably want to include those reliable sources. This will give the reader some comfort with the credibility of your writing.

Resources:

This is an optional page. I don't include it in every one of my books because they differ in nature. (This book is one in which I cite a number of different resources, so I'm including such a page.)

About the Author:

Another optional page important in building an audience for your future works is an "About the Author" page – a brief autobiography including some of your background, your experience, and what qualifies you as an expert if that's what you're claiming to be. It can also be a place for you to promote your future books. Or you may choose to promote your current and future books on a separate page altogether.

Index:

Another optional page is an Index page, and the decision to do an Index page would be driven by the complexity of the information you're presenting. In some cases where you have a complex subject with a lot of detailed information, it would be helpful to the reader to have an Index page.

Miscellaneous information:

Don't forget to include links to your blog, website and your Facebook page.

And for goodness sake, don't forget to include some type of offer. You don't have to wait 'til the end of the book to do this; you can do it at the front of the book (i.e., you're offering a free video or a special tool that would further help the reader).

If you do choose to promote an offer, do it with taste. And make sure that every other sentence, paragraph or chapter doesn't include some type of offer which can leave a "bad taste" in your reader's mind. You want them to keep reading and be enticed and enthralled; not closing the book and dumping it into the wastebasket due to your promotional overkill.

A warning: I'd encourage you not to overdo the sales pitch. It's okay to promote your offer and your links. But if the reader feels that's superior to the information in the book (in other words, they feel your real motivation is to try to sell them something else and not deliver quality information) they're not going to appreciate your book. They probably won't leave you a good review, and in many cases will leave you a bad review. So don't over-sell.

One of the big advantages to writing a book is it's a great way to generate leads for your other goods and services. Many of our subscribers came to us as a result of reading one of my books, which is why it's important to deliver good content. If they find it useful, they're likely to seek you out for even more information.

CHAPTER 11

What's Next?

Woohoo! You're almost done!

The Cover

Next to a compelling title, the single-most important factor in selling a book is a professional cover.
There are many amateur covers on Amazon.com,
and it's easy to see the difference. Occasionally a book
that has an amateur cover will become popular, but that's
typically not the case. If you look at Amazon's Top 100 in
any category, it's rare to find an amateur cover.

A well-designed cover will cost a little bit of money, but
it will be paid back many, many times over. (My graphic
designer, Joni McPherson, has created some of the very
best covers I've ever seen. And I invite you to check out her
contact information on the Resources page).

Copyrighting Your Material

Of course you'll want to copyright your work. The current U.S. law automatically extends copyright protection to every work as soon as it's created. Again, this book is not meant to give legal advice on copyright law. But I will inform you that even though you're given protection at the moment of creation, your enforcement and future ability to protect that copyright is strongly improved whenever you register the copyright with www.copyright.gov.

The fee is about $35 if you do it yourself, and it's a fairly simple application. However, if you're too busy you could outsource it to a copyright attorney at any one of the freelance websites.

I'd strongly encourage you to register the copyright of your book, especially if Amazon or one of the other booksellers questions whether you own the work (which has happened to me). Pointing them to a copyright registration will settle the matter immediately.

Convert and Upload Your Book

One of the first steps once your book is completed is to convert it to an eBook and upload it. Again, this can be done easily using freelancers. Some websites that sell eBooks also have software built into the sites that will convert them for you (i.e., www.Smashwords.com).

Once your eBook is converted (you'll need a .mobi version for Amazon and .epub for all the others), the interfaces of most retailers take just a few minutes to navigate.

You'll want to also take advantage of the CreateSpace opportunity (www.createspace.com is a subsidiary of Amazon). Once you've uploaded your eBook you can hire a freelancer to convert it into a format for printing, which is a simple process of creating a special print-ready PDF document. (We use a great freelancer at www.elance.com. Look for **Rosamond G.**)You then upload that PDF document to CreateSpace and voila! You now have a paperback version of your book.

CreateSpace doesn't charge you a penny up front for their services (there is a one-time $25 charge if you want expanded distribution to libraries and such). They print your book on demand as it's sold, and pay you a healthy royalty on each sale.

Even though eBooks have surpassed print books at Amazon.com, there's still a large marketplace for paperbacks and it's a profit stream you don't want to miss. The cost of formatting and tweaking your eBook cover to a print book is a small investment you should recoup quickly after making the paperback available (assuming, of course, you're selling a decent amount of eBooks).

Another advantage to using this strategy is that Amazon.com – since they own CreateSpace – seems to give some preference to my paperbacks I have listed with CreateSpace. They have on a number of occasions dramatically discounted the price by 25, 30, and even 40%, thereby making it more attractive to the buyer. And yet they never cut my commissions, keeping my royalties at the same level as if it were selling for full price (another strong point for utilizing the CreateSpace opportunity).

Perhaps the biggest benefit of uploading to CreateSpace is you get the opportunity to see your work in the flesh. eBooks are great informational vehicles and I'm a big believer in them, but it doesn't top the satisfaction of holding your own book in your hands!

Promote Your Book

Promote, promote, promote! Again, this is outside the purview of this book. But it's a necessity if you expect to have a popular book that will generate income over a long period of time. There are a number of amazing works that will never be known because their author or publisher never promoted the book, and will never achieve any type of real following.

There are wonderful marketing tools on the Internet, and some great programs that can help you learn how to promote your book. Promotion is one of the key concepts we teach in our Getting Rich With eBooks program, and there are any number of other sources of this information on the Web.

Now What?

Finally as we wrap this up, I want to encourage you that when you're done with your first book and you've cracked that bottle of champagne – or however you choose to celebrate (and you *should* celebrate because you've achieved something that few people will achieve, and you've done something you should be very proud of accomplishing) – you shouldn't wait too long to do it again.

Once you've learned this process it's like any other habit. As I said earlier, it's no different than learning to ride a bicycle. Once you've conquered how to do it the first time, it will be easier by far the second time, and the third time will be even easier than the second.

Let me give you some motivation to do it and keep doing it: One of my books has generated monthly royalties for almost ten years since my words went on paper and were published. I have done very little – and in many years absolutely nothing – to generate that income. Nonetheless, the royalty checks have continued to come, and I expect them to continue for years to come.

One of my primary motivations, besides wanting to communicate to my audience through the medium of books, has been to create a recurring source of income that provides a quality life for my family, whether it be retirement income, college education for my grandchildren, or for any number of reasons.

So I would encourage you to look at each book you have inside you as an annuity that can create income for you and your family over the years.

I congratulate you for having done your book this weekend. And if you haven't done it this weekend there's always next weekend. The main thing is to make the commitment to yourself that you're going to do it and then take the action to do it.

I <u>know you can do this</u>! I hope you keep me abreast of your progress, and when you publish your first book you'll drop me a line.

Until then, this is Vic Johnson ... and thank you!

Urgent Plea!

Thank you for purchasing my master's book!
It will really help life around here. Would you please
help Vic (and me) and go back to the site where you
purchased this book and leave your feedback.
He needs your feedback to make the
next version better. Arf! Arf!

Resources

- Amazon Spy Tool: http://getfreshkey.com

- Book Covers and Graphic Design:
  http://mcphersongraphics.com

- Copyright registration http://www.copyright.gov

- Freelancers: http://eLance.com (For print book
  conversion look for **Rosamond G.**)

- Google Alerts: http://www.google.com/alerts

- Google Keyword Ideas:
  http://adwords.google.com (you're looking for the
  keyword tool)

- Google Trends: http://www.google.com/trends/

- Ideas for Powerful Titles:
  http://ezee.info/405-ideas

• Logitech USB headset can be found at Amazon.com and others

• Mindmapping Software: http://www.mindjet.com

• Popular Topics on ClickBank: http://www.cbtrends.com

• Recording/Editing Software: http://audacity.sourceforge.net

• Title and Keyword Ideas: http://freekeywords.wordtracker.com/keyword-questions

• Transcription and Editing: http://thewritemojo.com

• WordPress and Website Design and Development http://watershedstudio.com

• Yahoo! Answers: http://answers.yahoo.com

About the Author

Twelve years ago Vic Johnson was totally unknown in the personal development field. Since that time he's created six of the most popular personal development sites on the Internet. One of them, www. AsAManthinketh.net has given away over 400,000 copies of James Allen's classic book. Three of them are listed in the top 5% of websites in the world (English language).

This success came despite the fact that he and his family were evicted from their home 16 years ago and the next year his last automobile was repossessed. His story of redemption and victory has inspired thousands around the world as he has taught the powerful principles that created incredible wealth in his life and for many others.

Today he serves more than 300,000 subscribers from virtually every country in the world. He's become an internationally known expert in goal-achieving, and has hosted his own TV show, *Goals 2 Go*, on TSTN.

His book, *13 Secrets of World Class Achievers,* is the

number one goal-setting book at both the Kindle store and Apple iBookstore.

Another best seller, *Day by Day with James Allen,* has sold more than 75,000 copies and has been translated into Japanese, Czech, Slovak and Farsi.

Vic's three-day weekend seminar event, *Claim Your Power Now*, has attracted such icons as Bob Proctor, Jim Rohn, Denis Waitley and many others.

His websites include:

GettingRichWitheBooks.com

AsAManThinketh.net

Goals2Go.com

MyDailyInsights.com

VicJohnson.com

ClaimYourPowerNow.com

LaurenzanaPress.com

How to Get a Good Audio Recording

(Or How to Prevent Your Transcriptionist
from Committing Harikari)
by Mary Jo Stresky
http://thewritemojo.com

I f you're going to be doing interviews on a regular basis, you should purchase a portable hand-held digital or desktop recorder.

The recordings can be downloaded to your computer in .wav or MP3 format, and emailed to your transcriptionist via many free programs (YouSendIt, FileSendIt, ShareFile, FTP, etc.).

If you must use mini, macro or standard tapes, make sure you do a test recording to assure the machine is running well, the tape is not damaged, and all extraneous noise, hisses, scratches have been eliminated. You want a CLEAN transcription for your transcriptionist. The harder they have to listen, the longer the transcription takes (which costs you more in the end). A bad recording can cause dropped critical information, or skewed statements because the transcriptionist has to guess what's being said.

With people's busy schedules it's sometimes impossible to get them in the best situation (i.e., a quiet room one-on-one). If you have to interview them while they're traveling, please explain that you need to get the best audio possible. Make arrangements for a time when they're alone in their office, a hotel room, at home, etc. Encourage them to use a landline (no cellphone), and stay off the speaker. They need to speak directly into the phone to get a quality recording.

Today's fast-paced individuals speak 260+ words on average per minute which means listening...relistening...relistening. The quality of transcription returned is dependent upon the audio quality, elimination of noises, the speaker's verbal ability, and where the microphone is placed (critical!). A good rule-of-thumb is to have the interviewee put their thumb on their chin and splay their hand. The end of the pinky is a good distance to place the hand-held or table-top microphone.

Why go through all the trouble of interviewing someone if you can't get the best returned documents possible? Following are a few tips to assure a quality audio:

If in a room:

• Lock the door so no one can interrupt the session.

• Put the phone on Do Not Disturb; or ask your assistant not to interrupt.

• Make sure the microphone is approximately 6" to 10" from the person's mouth. Too far away you can't hear; too close it becomes muffled.

• Do your due diligence. Research everything you can about the person before going into the interview on the Internet, or from their colleagues, family members, friends – whoever would be appropriate. Send them emails ahead of time asking pertinent pre-interview questions, or ask them what topics they would like to discuss.

• From there build your list of questions and study them before the interview. If you're disorganized and stumble through your thought processes, it can be confusing and uncomfortable for your interviewee who can lose their focus. You'll both lose momentum in the conversation and forget critical issues; therefore, you want a smooth-flowing interview.

If on a phone:

- PLEASE! If at all possible make sure you're both on a landline phone. **NO** cellphones, **NO** speaker phones. It's a nightmare trying to hear the interviewee as there's often too much outside interference, dropped words, scratching, etc.

- Encourage them to find a quiet place where they can be reached. If they have to be in a car, encourage them to pull over so they're not distracted; plus it eliminates car noise on the cellphone.

If in public:

- It's almost impossible to filter out all the clanking, banging, people's chatter, street noises, etc., on a recording (think of being at a restaurant where you can barely hear your partner and you miss much of the conversation. Painful, isn't it?) Be kind to your transcriptionist and make every effort that this doesn't happen.

- If you have to meet in public, please don't do this outside as street noise makes a quality audio very difficult. Try to get a table inside as far away from the kitchen as possible (hopefully in a corner far from the maddening crowd). Tip the waiter for the quietest one if you have to. It'll be worth it.

• Make sure the microphones (hopefully you'll each have one) are as close to you and your interviewee's mouths as possible (the six-inch rule).

How to conduct a good interview:

• If possible sit face-to-face so you won't watch each other speaking. Lip reading is a sure road to forgetting what you have to say as you'll concentrate more on the mole on their upper lip than their words.

• If possible make sure you both are using mics. (Quite often the interviewee will have a microphone, but the interviewer is sitting back and will be inaudible.) If not, have both of you sit as close to the mic as possible; otherwise, neither of you will be clear and your questions will be muffled.

• Don't interrupt the interviewee. Sometimes it's necessary to keep the train of thought flowing (especially if they ramble or you're needing clarification on a point); but wait to interject till a pause in the conversation. Too much information is lost when people constantly talk over each other.

• Write down any questions that arise while the interviewee is talking, then ask them during a pause in thought. Nothing is worse than when the interviewee is trying to think of the right things to say and is constantly interrupted. It causes break in thought and speech stuttering, they can't make a cohesive thought, and pertinent information is lost. Interruptions prevent gems from surfacing (it's like having a great dream but you don't write it down, and it drives you crazy that you can't remember it).

Your interviewee is giving their time, not the other way around. So be respectful, give them credibility, and don't make it about you. Otherwise, what's the point?